THE WOMEN'S SUFFRAGE MOVEMENT

Molly Housego & Neil R. Storey

SHIRE PUBLICATIONS

Published in Great Britain in 2016 by Shire Publications Ltd, part of Bloomsbury Publishing Plc
PO Box 883, Oxford, OX1 9PL, UK
1385 Broadway, 5th Floor, New York, NY 10018, USA.
E-mail: shire@shirebooks.co.uk   www.shirebooks.co.uk

A CIP catalogue record for this book is available from the British Library.

Shire Library no. 662.   ISBN-13: 978 0 74781 089 6

Molly Housego and Neil Storey have asserted their rights under the Copyright, Designs and Patents Act, 1988, to be identified as the authors of this book.

Designed by Myriam Bell Design, UK
Typeset in Perpetua and Gill Sans.
Printed in China through World Print Ltd.

16 17 18 19 20   12 11 10 9 8 7 6 5 4 3

COVER IMAGE
Suffragettes celebrate the release of Edith New and Mary Leigh from Holloway Prison on 22 August 1908, as depicted in *Le Petit Journal*.

TITLE PAGE IMAGE
The kitten roars, 'I want my Vote'. This postcard can be seen as both pro- and anti-women's suffrage, but was commonly sent between Women's Social and Political Union members and sympathisers in *c.* 1908.

CONTENTS PAGE IMAGE
A Votes for Women sash.

IMAGE ACKNOWLEDGEMENTS
Geoff Coulton, page 17; Simon Butler, page 23; Imperial War Museum, pages 13 and 41; Library of Congress, pages 9, 10, 14 (bottom left), 18, 19, 20, 38, 41 (top); Manchester Libraries, page 4; Mary Evans Picture Library, cover and pages 18, 22 (bottom right), 39, 55; Museum of London, pages 3, 21, 22 (bottom left), 25 (bottom right), 26, 30, 35 (bottom left), 43 (bottom); Topfoto, page 16 (top).

All other images are from the author's collection.

Shire Publications is supporting the Woodland Trust, the UK's leading woodland conservation charity, by funding the dedication of trees.

VOTES FOR WOMEN

CONTENTS

ORIGINS OF THE WOMEN'S SUFFRAGE MOVEMENT

Cavalry charge to disperse the open-air meeting of the Manchester Patriotic Union on St Peter's Field, Manchester, on 16 August 1819. Over six hundred people were injured and fifteen died as a result of the incident, which became known as the Peterloo Massacre.

UNIVERSAL SUFFRAGE, IN OTHER WORDS the right to vote, was not a right enjoyed by all British people in the nineteenth century. The right was limited to men with considerable property or land: in 1831 just 4,500 men out of a population of more than 2.6 million people were entitled to vote in parliamentary elections. The situation had also become farcical because the electoral areas were out of date and un-reformed – the new industrial cities such as Birmingham, Leeds and Manchester had no members to represent them in Parliament, while some 'rotten boroughs', such as Dunwich on the coast of Suffolk, once a bustling town and port but reduced through erosion and storm to a village with a population of thirty-two in 1831, were still sending two MPs to Westminster.

Pressure had come in the late eighteenth century from radical reformers such as Thomas Paine (the author of *Rights of Man*, 1791) and continued throughout the nineteenth century, notably during the 1830s and '40s from the Chartists, who demanded 'Universal Manhood Suffrage' as part of their six-point charter, and from the less radical Reform League in the 1860s. These waves of pressure for parliamentary reform resulted in three main Reform Acts in 1832, 1867 and 1884, which extended the franchise first to all householders who paid rates in 'constituency boroughs' and then to 'county constituencies'. As a result, some 6 million men (almost 60 per cent of the adult male population) joined the voting registers but women were still denied any vote at all.

Appeals and arguments for widening the franchise to include women can also be traced back to the eighteenth century, when Mary Wollstonecraft published *A Vindication of the Rights of Women* (1792), a year after Paine's *Rights of Man*. Female suffrage was advocated by the respected philosopher and reformer Jeremy Bentham in his book *A Plan for Parliamentary Reform* (1818), and was also argued for as part of a wider platform of universal suffrage by radical orators such as Henry Hunt. Hunt stood for equal laws, equal rights, annual parliaments, universal suffrage and the secret ballot (a legend he would later emblazon upon the labels of the boot-blacking bottles he manufactured). He was asked by the Manchester Patriotic Union to address a rally of over sixty thousand on St Peter's Field, Manchester, on 16 August 1819; on the platform with him were a number of others who were due to speak for reform, and beside them was a woman carrying a banner bearing the legend 'Female Reformers of Roynton – Let us die like men and not be sold like slaves'. Shortly after the arrival of Hunt, local magistrates, disturbed by the enthusiastic greeting he had received, ordered his arrest and the dispersal of the crowd. This order was carried out with extreme violence by the military, including a cavalry charge with sabres drawn. Fifteen people died and over six hundred were injured in the incident, which became known as the Peterloo Massacre – it was often recalled by those who fought for suffrage over the ensuing years with the cry of 'Remember Peterloo!'

In 1832 the so-called 'Great Reform Act' had explicitly excluded all women from voting in national elections by using the term 'male' rather than 'person' in its wording. Henry Hunt had been elected member for Preston in 1830 and had argued that any woman who was single, a taxpayer and had sufficient property should be allowed to vote both before and after this legislation had been passed, and in response to the Reform Act presented the first petition in support of women's suffrage to Parliament in 1832. The petition was, however, mocked and Hunt was exposed to antagonism for his efforts.

Lydia Becker
(1827–90), founder
of the National
Society for
Women's Suffrage,
the first national
group to campaign
for women's right
to vote.

Although the issue of women's rights and changing roles in society was discussed by both men and women (the Chartists, for example, argued for universal suffrage), and some small groups were created (such as the Sheffield Association for Female Franchise in 1851), female suffrage did not attract major national attention again until 1865 when John Stuart Mill promised that he would introduce a women's suffrage amendment to the 1867 Reform Bill. In direct support of this a number of high-profile feminist campaigners such as Barbara Bodichon (the author of *Women and Work*, 1858), Jessie Boucherett (co-founder with Adelaide Ann Proctor and Bodichon of the Society for Promoting the Employment of Women in 1859), Emily Davies (author of *The Higher Education of Women*, 1866), Elizabeth Garrett (the first woman to qualify as a doctor) and Helen Taylor (the step-daughter of John Stuart Mill) drew up a petition demanding the enfranchisement of all householders irrespective of sex. Signed by almost 1,500 women, the petition was presented to Parliament by John Stuart Mill and Henry Fawcett – two of the few MPs sympathetic to their cause.

The Second Reform Bill did enfranchise many working-class and middle-income men but when Mill proposed the extension of the franchise to women the motion was defeated by 194 votes to 73. Times, however, were changing. Women were heartened by the fact that there had been support for the enfranchisement of women; moreover, influential women from higher social spheres were taking an interest in the rights of women. A number of women's suffrage groups were created in Manchester, Birmingham, Bristol, Edinburgh, Ireland and London, and it soon became apparent that the groups being established across the United Kingdom could combine and have a far more powerful voice. The National Society for Women's Suffrage, formed by Lydia Becker on 6 November 1867, became the first national group to campaign for women's right to vote.

Following the creation of this first national organisation, disagreements over strategy beleaguered the group. The London suffrage group was a typical example: one faction, led by Helen Taylor, wanted a women-only committee; Barbara Bodichon argued for the involvement of men. Both factions argued passionately and articulately but such internal wrangling only weakened the thrust of the group. The society lost credibility and other spin-off groups

The socialists' red flag being wrested from socialist leader Helen Taylor during the Bloody Sunday riot, Trafalgar Square, 13 November 1887.

Social campaigner Annie Besant (1847–1933), whose 'White Slavery in London' article prompted the London match-girls' strike in 1888.

soon emerged, along with other groups that supported other relevant issues, such as the Ladies' National Association and its campaigns against the Contagious Diseases Act (an Act that blamed prostitutes for venereal disease, rather than the men who used them).

Other societies, such as the Women's Liberal Associations (the first of which was formed in 1881) and the Conservative Primrose League (founded in 1883), were formed without a specific women's suffrage agenda; these demonstrated women's competence in the political arena and consequently brought female suffrage closer to acceptance. Women were particularly prominent among socialists during the late nineteenth century. Annie Besant came to prominence for her work in drawing attention to the plight of the unemployed in London and was one of those blamed for incensing the crowd during the Bloody Sunday riot in 1887. But Besant will be best remembered for her concern for the improvement of working conditions in London, particularly the horrendous impact of white phosphorus upon the

Eleanor Marx
(1855–98),
daughter of the
philosopher and
sociologist Karl
Marx, was a
socialist
campaigner, a fine
orator and the
author of *The
Factory Hell* (1885)
and *The Woman
Question* (1886).

health of the employees of Bryant & May's match factory. Her 'White Slavery in London' article (published in *The Link* on 23 June 1888) became one of the catalysts for the London match-girls' strike in the same year. Contrary to popular belief, Annie did not lead the strike – the workers came out of their own accord – but she helped with negotiations at meetings with the management and campaigned passionately for the match girls' cause.

Another socialist campaigner and fine orator was Eleanor Marx, daughter of Karl Marx and author of *The Factory Hell* (1885) and *The Woman Question* (1886). Marx had also become involved in the match-girls' strike of 1888 and played a valuable role in arguing the case for the plight of the London dock workers in her own right in 1889. Clementina Black had been an activist in the Consumers' League, which appealed to customers to put pressure on employers who paid very low wages to women. She then went on to become one of the founders of the Women's Trade Union Association (WTUA) with her friend Eleanor Marx. Five years later this association merged with the Women's Industrial Council, retaining the name of the WIC, many of whose members were also active in the suffrage movement.

Despite the eloquence and passion of the women coming to prominence over social and political issues, there were still detractors, both male and female, who for a variety of reasons based on political, religious or personal beliefs considered it unbecoming for women to have the vote or to campaign for it. Beatrice Webb summed up these opinions when she wrote of Annie Besant:

> I felt interested in that powerful woman, with her blighted wifehood and motherhood and her thirst for power and defence of the world. I heard her speak, the only woman I have ever known who is a real orator, who has the gift of public persuasion. But to see her speaking made me shudder. It is not womanly to thrust yourself before the world.

Despite its detractors, the women's suffrage campaign strove on, but disagreements over strategy and political allegiances also continued until

1888, when the main suffrage movement split in two, resulting in the creation of the Central National Society for Women's Suffrage and (confusingly) the similarly named Central Committee of the National Society for Women's Suffrage. Again there were disagreements over strategy and political allegiance and this time the spin-off group was the more radical Women's Franchise League (WFL), created by Emmeline Pankhurst and her barrister husband Richard in 1889. The WFL supported equal rights for women in the areas of divorce and inheritance, advocated trade unionism and sought alliances with socialist organisations, but these views did not always sit comfortably with all its members. The groups, especially those who felt acrimonious after the split, soon indulged in public mud-slinging: the more conservative groups from the NSWS criticised the WFL as being the 'extreme left wing' of the movement, while the WFL ridiculed them as the 'Spinster Suffrage Party'. When both Emmeline and Richard Pankhurst heckled the speaker at a large meeting organised by Lydia Becker at

Millicent Garrett Fawcett (1847–1929), first President of the National Union of Women's Suffrage Societies.

St James's Hall it proved to be the tipping point; a number of WFL resignations followed as members wished to dissociate themselves from such behaviour, and the group dissolved after about twelve months of existence.

As the nineteenth century drew to a close a new attempt to bring together the disparate women's suffrage groups was attempted in 1897, when no fewer than seventeen women's groups joined together to form the National Union of Women's Suffrage Societies (NUWSS), with Millicent Fawcett elected as its first President. Fawcett was a moderate campaigner who distanced herself from militancy, believing that the actions of the likes of the Pankhursts did more harm than good for the women's suffrage cause. The Pankhursts, however, felt they had not done enough.

A NEW CENTURY AND
A NEW DIRECTION

A S THE NINETEENTH CENTURY DREW TO A CLOSE Emmeline and Richard Pankhurst had become prominent activists in the women's suffrage movement. Emmeline was born on 15 July 1858 (although she always celebrated her birthday on 14 July – Bastille Day), the eldest girl in a family of ten surviving children of Robert and Sophie Goulden of Moss Side, Manchester. Her family was middle-class; her father was co-founder of a cotton-printing and bleach works at Seedley; they had not only a family home near the factory but also a second home on the Isle of Man. Born at a time when Manchester was dedicated to free trade and it was widely believed there that businesses should be free from government interference, her family had a long history of political activism. Robert's father was present at the Peterloo Massacre and his mother had worked with the Anti-Corn Law League in the 1840s. Emmeline's parents took a great interest in politics – her father served for a number of years on Salford Town Council and both parents were keen supporters of universal suffrage (votes for both men and women) and involved all their children in social activism from an early age. Books such as *Uncle Tom's Cabin*, which so powerfully revealed new perspectives on humanity and social justice, were a common source of bedtime stories for all the Pankhurst children; indeed, one of Emmeline's earliest political memories was collecting money at a bazaar for the newly freed slaves of the United States.

Emmeline was sent to the École Normale de Neuilly in France at the age of fifteen, not only to receive a rounded education but also to be groomed in the manners of a lady. She returned to Manchester at the age of nineteen as a confident young lady with an educated flair for personal presentation. Her good deportment, grace and refined dress sense would always remain her hallmark – Christabel recalled a guest at their Russell Square home describe Emmeline as 'a living flame. As active as a bit of quicksilver, as glistening, as enticing. Emmeline Pankhurst was very beautiful. She looked like the model of Burne-Jones' pictures – slender, willowy, with the exquisite features of one of the saints of the great impressionist.'

Opposite:
Mrs Emmeline
Pankhurst (1858–
1929).

A short while after Emmeline's return from school in France she saw Dr Richard Pankhurst speaking at a political meeting. A doctor of law, he was a formidable barrister with a fine ginger beard, known to many as 'the Red Doctor' not only for his distinctive facial hair but also for his political inclinations to the far left of the Liberal Party. Dr Pankhurst was already a well-known advocate of women's suffrage and other causes, including freedom of speech and education reform. Despite his being over twenty years her senior, Emmeline was smitten; they shared the same social conscience and very soon he was writing in terms of endearment to her, pledging that in their life together 'Every struggling cause shall be ours.' They married on 18 December 1879 and soon began their family with the birth of Christabel Harriette in 1880, followed by Estelle Sylvia (always known as Sylvia) in 1882, Francis Henry ('Frank') in 1884 and Adela Constantia in 1885.

Richard Pankhurst was determined his wife should not become 'a household machine', so a servant was hired to attend to the children, freeing Emmeline to continue her work with the NUWSS. The Pankhurst children were also raised with strong social consciences and political awareness; they accompanied their parents during canvassing, helped to collect money at political meetings and grew up seeing their mother as an ardent campaigner for women's suffrage as well as a supporter of other high-profile causes such as the free speech meeting in Trafalgar Square that ended in the notorious 'Bloody Sunday' riot in 1887, and the Bryant & May match-girls' strike in 1888.

The Pankhursts had residences in both Manchester and London, maintaining a presence in this latter location so they could be within the hub of politics and Parliament. Using what little savings they had, Richard and Emmeline bought a small shop on Hampstead Road in North London and began selling fancy goods. Sadly, the shop was not a success; the goods proved to be too high-quality and expensive for the local clientele. Tragedy struck with the death of young Frank of diphtheria in 1888. Both parents were distraught. Believing a faulty drainage system behind their house to be the cause of the illness, the Pankhursts moved to the more affluent and cleaner Russell Square. It was at this latter address that the Pankhursts entertained many prominent activists such as Annie Besant, William Morris, dock strike leaders John Burns and Tom Mann, Eleanor Marx – even the communist philosopher Prince Kropotkin was a guest at soirées over the years.

Tragically, just as the older Pankhurst girls were entering their late teens, their father died suddenly as a result of a gastric ulcer on 2 July 1898. Emmeline appeared strong and stoical but, as Christabel was to remark, the sadness that overcame her mother's face at the death of Richard never left her for the rest of her life. It seemed as though the loss of Richard drove Emmeline to fight on with renewed vigour, pushing for progress in the votes for women cause, and she brought her elder daughters with her.

SMOKING

The problem with the previous Women's Suffrage groups had been in-fighting and failure to agree on policies; Emmeline had been frustrated by their failure to progress for a long while, but when the memorial hall built in honour of Richard Pankhurst (and painted with murals at no cost by Sylvia) was to be used by an Independent Labour Party branch that did not admit women, an injustice against which Richard Pankhurst had always fought, Emmeline's mind was made up, and she declared: 'We must have an independent women's movement!' A group of women socialists joined Emmeline at her Manchester home on Nelson Street on 10 October 1903 and they resolved to approve a new group that would break away from the NUWSS and use direct action for their cause. The new group would have exclusively female membership and would live by the motto of 'Deeds not Words' in their campaign; this new organisation was the Women's Social and Political Union (WSPU).

Initially the fledgling WSPU was very similar to other women's franchise groups; its activities were non-violent and consisted of making public speeches and gathering signatures for petitions. Although free from party affiliations, the WSPU initially drew close alliances with the Independent Labour Party and spoke at a number of trade union and political meetings. Labour MP Keir Hardie was prominent in his support for the women's suffrage cause and was instrumental in bringing in the first bill for the enfranchisement of women in the twentieth century. The bill drew a great deal of attention and some three hundred women from a number of interested groups including the NUWSS and WSPU were drawn to the lobby of the House of Commons when the bill was read on 12 May 1905. But the Enfranchisement Bill was the Second Order of the day and followed a First Order measure to compel carts to carry a rear light at night. The opponents to women's suffrage strung out the debate with waffle and filibustering, so when the Second Order to discuss the Women's Franchise Bill was opened the usual opposing debates were proffered and the bill was talked out.

Emmeline was incensed by this parliamentary chicanery and expressing her disgust by rallying many of the women who had attended outside the Parliament building. A number of NUWSS members who had been present made their exit but still a good number gathered around. Just as veteran women's campaigner Elizabeth Wolstenholme Elmy began to speak, police officers intervened and ordered the crowd to disperse. Emmeline was not intimidated by the interruption and responded by asking where they should meet instead. A police inspector advised them to go to Broad Sanctuary, near Westminster Abbey. His suggestion was clearly given in haste and in an effort

Below: An early illustrative poster points out the disparities between those who were entitled to vote and, significantly, those who were excluded.

Below right: *Punch* cartoon, 'The Dignity of the Franchise', first published on 10 May 1905, and later reproduced on pamphlets by the Women's Social and Political Union.

THE DIGNITY OF THE FRANCHISE.

to get the crowd of women away, for under the Metropolitan Police Act of 1839 demonstrations were forbidden in the vicinity of the Houses of Parliament while a sitting was taking place. Emmeline believed this act to have been a successful demonstration of how militancy can draw the attention of the media and regarded this event as 'the first militant action of the WSPU'.

The WSPU had drawn to its ranks a number of new members who were willing to take part in more militant actions in the name of their cause. Among them was Annie Kenney, the only working-class woman to become a leading figure in the WSPU. Kenney had been born at Saddleworth in Yorkshire in 1879 and had worked in a local cotton mill since the age of ten; she had lost a finger when it was torn off by a spinning bobbin. Involved in union activities and furthering her education by self-study, she became actively involved in the WSPU after hearing Christabel Pankhurst speak at the Oldham Clarion Vocal Club in 1905. Later that same year, on Friday 13 October, she joined Christabel at an election meeting held in the Manchester Free Trade Hall where Sir Edward Grey and Winston Churchill were speaking for the Liberal cause. During a pause in questions Kenney asked Churchill, 'If you are elected, will you do your best to make women's suffrage a Government measure?' Neither Churchill nor Grey offered a reply. Christabel then unfurled a banner emblazoned with the words 'Votes for Women', the lecture hall went into uproar, and order was restored only with the intervention of the Chief Constable, who suggested the women put the question in writing. The situation calmed down but as the meeting was about to be adjourned Annie Kenney unfurled the banner again, and asked directly, 'Will the Liberal Government give women the vote?' The room erupted again and this time stewards and police officers removed Christabel and Kenney from the hall. In the course of this eviction Christabel spat in the faces of Superintendent Watson and Inspector Mather, whom she also struck in the mouth. When outside, the cries and shrieks of the two women drew quite a crowd on South Street but as they attempted to address those gathered outside both women were promptly arrested and charged with disorderly behaviour. When brought before the Manchester Police Court, Christabel used the situation as a platform for her cause, stating: 'My conduct in the Free Trade Hall and outside was meant as a

Annie Kenney (1879–1953), the only working-class woman to become a leading figure in the WSPU.

Annie Kenney and Christabel Pankhurst with their banner (1905).

protest against the legal position of women today. We cannot make any orderly protest because we have not the means whereby citizens may do such a thing; we have not a vote; and so long as we have not votes we must be disorderly. There is no other way whereby we can put forward our claims to political justice.'

When the magistrates then retired to consider their decision, the ladies, defiant to the end, produced a 'Votes for Women' banner and hung it on the dock rail; it was rapidly removed before the return of the magistrates. The sentence handed down was a fine of 10s 6d for Christabel's assault upon a police officer, while both women received a fine of 5s, or three days for causing an obstruction. Both women refused to pay the fine and were imprisoned, these events and, most importantly, the cause of women's suffrage receiving national news coverage. A meeting was held at the same Free Trade Hall as the protest to welcome the imprisoned activists out of prison and the hall was packed to capacity with an audience ready to listen to what they had to say.

Flora Drummond (foreground) and Annie Kenney, expounding their 'Votes for Women' arguments as they are escorted away from a protest in front of 10 Downing Street on 9 March 1906.

Further interruptions by suffragettes at political meetings ensued and soon all members of the Liberal government were suffering heckles and disturbances at their public meetings. Disruption was soon extended to other events and organisations that, in the eyes of the WSPU, appeared to endorse male authority, notably the Church. Disruptions and protests soon became widespread at both Church of England and nonconformist services in cathedrals, churches and chapels.

By the spring of 1906 the methods of the NUWSS and WSPU had become sharply contrasted: the NUWSS maintained their peaceful pressure for the cause as women suffragists while the militant actions of WSPU members led to the *Daily Mail* condescendingly naming them 'suffragettes' – a name they proudly accepted and adopted. The WSPU was, however, still perceived as a pressure group with more enthusiasm than organisation and it was Keir Hardy who brought an invaluable asset to the WSPU when he introduced Emmeline Pankhurst to the wealthy social activist Emmeline Pethick-Lawrence and her successful businessman husband Frederick, who owned the left-wing evening newspaper *The Echo*. Mrs Pethick-Lawrence certainly proved her loyalty to the cause: within months of joining the WSPU she served a sentence of six months' imprisonment for attempting to make a speech in the lobby of the House of Commons (the first of six terms of imprisonment she would serve for her political activities). Very soon the dynamic partnership of the WSPU was established: Emmeline and Christabel dealt with leadership and policy while the Pethick-Lawrences worked as business managers for the WSPU, using their formidable marketing skills and contacts to help promote the movement and raise funds for a national campaign.

The WSPU was soon operating from a spare room at the Pethick-Lawrence residence at 4 Clement's Inn, the Strand, London, and took over the entire lower floor of Clement's Inn when it became available in September 1906. In the wake of the mass media attention and the publicity skills of the Pethick-Lawrences, Emmeline was delighted to declare, 'We are at last recognized as a political party; we are now in the swim of politics, and are a political force.'

The WSPU movement gathered momentum but was increasingly frustrated in its attempts to get the message across. By 1907, fears of

MRS. PETHICK LAWRENCE
JOINT EDITOR OF "VOTES FOR WOMEN"
HONORARY TREASURER, NATIONAL WOMEN'S SOCIAL & POLITICAL UNION,
4 CLEMENT'S INN, W.C.

Emmeline Pethick-Lawrence (1867–1954) and her husband, Frederick, became the business and propaganda masterminds of the WSPU.

A suffragette being moved on by a pair of burly policemen.

disruption to political meetings and some religious services saw women banned from entry in many places. Some attempted to gain entry by arriving early and concealing themselves under stages, in adjacent rooms, in store cupboards or even among organ pipes, later revealing themselves and their banners, shouting slogans for the WSPU cause during the meeting. There were even instances of WSPU activists being lowered into public meeting halls from skylights!

Women attempting to make speeches or shout slogans on public streets or outside public buildings where political meetings were being held were also rapidly moved along. Many of these women had accepted they might be arrested; indeed many wanted to be, intent on being brought before a court, and made arrest as difficult as possible to draw maximum publicity. The police were only too aware of this. Many of the WSPU women were slight in build, and were frequently lifted up and physically carried away to custody by one or more burly policemen. In response to this the WSPU women took to chaining themselves to railings and similar fastenings, to hinder their removal.

Many of the WSPU women were slight in build and could be lifted up and carried to custody by one or more policemen. In response to this, suffragettes began chaining themselves to railings and similar fixed objects.

In the face of such dramatic events the continued campaign of the NUWSS fell into the shadow of the WSPU. The NUWSS did attempt to raise its profile, notably with the 'Mud March' of over three thousand women who marched through the muddy streets of London to advocate women's suffrage on 7 February 1907. But a few days later, on 13 February 1907, far greater media attention was given to the events that ensued from the first 'Women's Parliament', convened at Caxton Hall in London, with Emmeline Pankhurst presiding. A resolution expressing indignation that the women's suffrage cause had been excluded from the King's Speech for the opening of Parliament resulted in the cry of 'Rise up, Women!' from the platform; a voice cried 'Now!' in response and the women poured out on to the street with copies of the resolution in their hands, and headed for the Houses of Parliament. They were soon confronted by a body of mounted police riding up to them at a smart trot and the police did not stop as they rode through the procession, sending women fleeing to the pavements and doorways. The mounted police made a number of return passes and caused many of the women to retreat. Many more policemen joined the mêlée on foot but fifteen women managed to fight their way as far as the Strangers' Lobby of the House. They attempted to hold a meeting there, but were

Suffragettes march on the Houses of Parliament, c. 1910.

almost immediately arrested, as were many more outside. Order was eventually restored, Parliament Square was cleared of crowds and both mounted and foot police continued to guard the approaches to the House of Commons until the House rose at midnight. The following morning, fifty-seven women and two men were brought before Westminster Police Court in groups of two and three; many of them, including Christabel Pankhurst, chose prison rather than paying the fine. During the hearing the magistrate, Mr Curtis Bennett, toed the official line and would have no blame attached to the police for their actions in the dispersal of the procession, but the newspaper reportage of the event drew considerable public interest and, significantly, sympathy for the suffragette cause. Many suffragettes would also recall this incident with great bitterness, nor would it be the last time they would be so treated.

As the first conference of the WSPU approached in September 1907 a number of the influential women who had joined the WSPU, headed by Charlotte Despard and one of the WSPU's first five speech-makers, Teresa Billington Grieg, suggested there should be greater democracy in the organisation and increased autonomy for branches. A written constitution was drawn up, proposing annual conferences where there would be an election of officers by members, but Emmeline and Christabel Pankhurst would have none

Suffragettes protest outside London police courts, 1907.

of it and, in a carefully orchestrated and very public response to the suggestion, tore up the constitution in front of the conference delegates and threw it to the ground, condemning those who proposed it as conspirators in an attempted *coup d'état* against the movement's permanent commander-in-chief.

For some this was an unsurprising act by an autocratic leader but Emmeline had learned from bitter experience that division of purpose and disagreements within previous women's suffrage groups had weakened their efforts and lost them credibility. Emmeline saw to it that the governance of the WSPU was limited to her own family members, with herself in overall command. Those who had proposed the WSPU constitution and many of their supporters (about a fifth of the WSPU membership) went on to form their own group, the Women's Freedom League, while the remaining membership of the WSPU was left with no illusions: all members would be required to share Emmeline's single vision with unquestioning loyalty. There was to be no formal constitution — Emmeline and Christabel took the lead and anyone who disagreed with their policies or methods was not welcome in the ranks of the WSPU. In many ways these events gave even greater

Flora Drummond, an early stalwart, organiser and inspiring orator of the WSPU, was soon dubbed 'General' by the members; she was imprisoned nine times for the Votes for Women cause.

stability to the WSPU and the union forged ahead with renewed clarity in its aims and vigour in its initiatives to achieve them. In October 1907 the Pethick-Lawrences created the means of disseminating such messages and news of events from the WSPU to its members and supporters by establishing and co-editing the WSPU's own mass-circulation weekly newspaper, *Votes for Women*, which sold for 1d.

The year 1907 was to be marked by one significant gain: women were admitted to the register to vote in and stand for election to principal local authorities, but still they were not granted the vote in general elections.

The year 1908 was to be another significant one for the WSPU. It began with suffragettes promoting their cause to ministers attending a meeting of the Cabinet in Downing Street in January. As each minister simply brushed by the women, one of them, Miss Edith New, chained herself to the railings of No. 10 — as Midge Mackenzie related in *Shoulder to*

Shoulder (1975), 'both symbolically to express the political bondage of womanhood and for the very practical reason that this device would prevent her being dragged speedily away'. She was soon joined by another, a nurse named Olivia Smith. A taxi-cab then drove up and, as more constables rushed to the pavement-side door of the vehicle, Flora Drummond leapt out on the road side, sped round the policemen and dashed into No. 10! A number of ministers immediately fell upon her and she was rapidly ejected from the building. More arrests followed, as did more newspaper headlines. Even Emmeline was arrested the following month 'for obstruction' after attempting to take another bill to Parliament. Refusing to accept being bound over to keep the peace, she and the six other members of the delegation in court chose prison and spent six weeks inside. On the day of her release Emmeline addressed the first meeting of the WSPU to be held at the Royal Albert Hall.

The membership of the WSPU continued to grow and their first rally, held on 21 June 1908 and described in their publicity as a 'monster meeting', was known as 'Women's Sunday'. This event brought together thousands of suffragettes from all over the United Kingdom to march in seven processions through London, culminating in a rally at Hyde Park.

The spectacle of Women's Sunday was carefully planned with the importance and power of visual impact in mind. The orders of the day for the

Below: A Votes for Women rosette.

Below right: A selection of suffragette badges. The tin badge (top left), designed by Sylvia Pankhurst for the suffragette campaign, depicts a woman breaking free – stepping through a gate with iron bars and heavy chains, carrying a 'Votes for Women' streamer.

The 'Panko or Votes for Women' card game, with images designed by the *Punch* cartoonist E.T. Reed, was launched in 1909, with packs selling for 2 shillings each.

Celluloid photo portrait button badges of Emmeline Pankhurst and others, such as this one showing Christabel Pankhurst, sold for a penny to raise funds for the WSPU.

march were that it was to be a dignified parade but a 'riot of colour.' This element was brilliantly devised and orchestrated by Emmeline Pethick-Lawrence, with the corporate colours of the WSPU movement presented to the public for the first time at this event. Each colour was symbolic, as the chorus of the 'Purple, White and Green March' explained:

> Purple stands for the loyal heart
> Loyal to cause and King;
> White for purity, Green for hope,
> Bright hopes of Spring.

Mrs Pethick-Lawrence urged members participating in the parades to:

The first arrest (13 February 1908) of WSPU leader Emmeline Pankhurst in Victoria Street, London, on a charge of obstruction – for which she received six weeks in Holloway Prison.

Women's suffrage leaders and symbolic banners carried on the Women's Sunday processions, 21 June 1908.

Be guided by the colours in your choice of dress… we have seven hundred banners in purple, white and green. The effect will be very much lost unless the colours are carried out in the dress of every woman in the ranks. White or cream tussore should if possible be the dominant colour; the purple and green should be introduced where other colour is necessary… I wish I could impress upon every mind as deeply as I feel myself the importance of popularising the colours in every way open to us…

With an estimated half a million in attendance, Women's Sunday was a phenomenal success and suffragettes were urged to wear and display their colours at all times, especially if they were at large events and political meetings. The Pethick-Lawrences and businesses supportive of the WSPU cause then set about producing a vast array of goods in 'the colours', from the overt sashes, scarves, a wide array of pictorial and enamel badges and rosettes to crockery, hat pins, board and card games and even bicycles. There were also more subtle means of displaying

loyalty such as decorated buttons, handkerchiefs and jewellery set with stones of purple, white and green.

By 1909 there began to be regular mention of 'suffragette uniform'. This consisted of a 'short skirt' (this meant just off the ground but not revealing ankles) of purple or green to be worn with a white golf jersey and a simple hat of purple or green, with the purple, white and green sash worn over the right shoulder and fastened under the left arm. It was to be worn 'by all able to do so', on parades or at homecomings for suffragettes released from prison.

A panorama showing some of the thousands who attended the Women's Sunday open-air meeting at Hyde Park on 21 June 1908.

WSPU standard bearer Miss Daisy Dugdale carries 'the colours' as she leads the 'Rise Up Women!' procession in London, October 1908.

THE CAT AND MOUSE ACT

PASSED BY THE LIBERAL GOVERNMENT

THE LIBERAL CAT
ELECTORS VOTE AGAINST HIM!
KEEP THE LIBERAL OUT!

BUY AND READ 'THE SUFFRAGETTE' PRICE 1^{D.}

WOMEN'S SOCIAL & POLITICAL UNION - LINCOLN'S INN HOUSE KINGSWAY W.C.

DEEDS NOT WORDS

U NTIL THE CLOSE OF THE FIRST DECADE of the twentieth century, suffragette militant action had consisted primarily of disturbing political meetings and committing minor offences such as chalking and stencilling suffragette messages on walls and pavements and defacing coinage of the realm in circulation by stamping pennies with the slogan 'Votes for Women'. By 1909 suffragettes had made a number of marches and rushes on Parliament; chaining themselves to railings became a well-known tactic to prevent their rapid removal, but a number of more serious incidents had occurred, such as throwing stones at politicians' cars or at the windows of public halls where political meetings were being held. Suffragette Theresa Garnett even got close enough to deal a blow to Winston Churchill MP, President of the Board

Opposite:
The Prisoner's (Temporary Discharge of Ill Health) Act (1913), soon commonly known as the 'Cat and Mouse Act', granted the release of prisoners on hunger strike until they had recovered sufficiently; they would then be re-admitted to complete their sentence.

Left: Christabel Pankhurst addresses a rally in Trafalgar Square on 11 October 1908 to promote the WSPU's 'rush to Parliament' planned for 13 October.

Prime Minister Herbert Henry Asquith is waylaid by two suffragettes. They are attempting to draw from him a commitment for votes for women. November 1908.

Christabel Pankhurst, Flora Drummond and Emmeline Pankhurst in the dock of Bow Street Magistrates' Court, London, during their trial for sedition, charged with incitement to 'rush the House of Commons' in October 1908.

of Trade, with a dog whip at Bristol station, catching his face and denting his hat, crying 'You brute! Why don't you treat British women properly?' before she was hauled away by two plain-clothes detectives.

Despite having had unprecedented public attention, the women's suffrage movement's regular round of disruptions, disturbances, arrests and subsequent court appearances became tiresome to the media. The failure of the women's suffrage cause to gain any further ground in their appeals to get the matter discussed in Parliament led to Miss Wallace Dunlop entering the House of Commons on 5 July 1909 and stencilling a 'women's right to petition' notice upon the wall of St Stephen's Hall. Arrested and charged at Bow Street with 'wilful damage', she was sent in default of her fine to prison for one calendar month. Upon admittance to Holloway Prison, upon her own initiative she protested to then Home Secretary, Herbert Gladstone, that she should be placed in the first division of prisoners, as befitted one charged with a political offence, and 'would eat no food until this right was conceded'. After maintaining her fast for ninety-one hours she was released. The incident drew press attention and hunger strikes followed from other suffragettes when they were imprisoned.

The willingness of suffragettes to go to prison for their militant actions is satirised in 'Suffragettes at Home', from *Punch*, 14 April 1909.

A special medal was struck as a mark of recognition for those who served prison sentences for militancy and went on hunger strike. Produced in silver, with a suspension bar marked 'For Valour' and a ribbon of purple, white and green, the first of these medals were presented in St James's Hall, Great

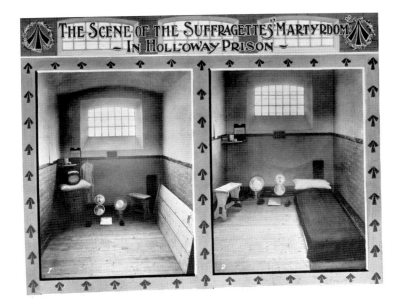

The imprisonment of suffragettes drew a great deal of media interest, especially the conditions and experiences they had while 'behind bars'.

Portland Street, in August 1909. Unwilling to have suffragettes martyr themselves in this way, the government's knee-jerk reaction was to introduce force feeding in September 1909. The hunger-striking suffragette prisoner would be frog-marched to a reinforced chair, bound in a sheet and lifted into a sitting position; her arms and legs would be held by prison wardresses and a nasal tube introduced by the prison doctor – through this she would be fed a liquid food. Comment was made in the press about this brutal treatment, although some correspondents, particularly in the letters columns, even tried to argue it was humane.

Discrimination was applied in deciding which prisoners were to be force fed and which were not. Authorities denied this was the case, so suffragette activist Lady Constance Bulwer-Lytton, who had already been imprisoned at Holloway under her real name and was not force fed 'for medical reasons', committed another criminal act in Liverpool in 1910 as a suffragette, but in disguise as a working-class London seamstress named Jane Warton. Sure enough she was force fed; the experiences she had to relate, including some all-too-vivid accounts of force feeding, were lapped up by the media and

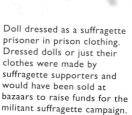

Doll dressed as a suffragette prisoner in prison clothing. Dressed dolls or just their clothes were made by suffragette supporters and would have been sold at bazaars to raise funds for the militant suffragette campaign.

The Holloway Prison brooch, comprising a portcullis symbol of the House of Commons, superimposed with a broad arrow (typical of those marked on prison clothing), embellished with purple, white and green enamel representing the WSPU. It was designed by Sylvia Pankhurst and presented to suffragette ex-prisoners and worn by them with great pride.

Hunger-strike medal presented to the suffragette Florence Haig on her release from prison in 1912. The bars represent other sentences for militant activities.

Purposeful and proud, suffragettes walk away after release from their incarceration in Holloway Prison, having served their sentences for militant actions during the 'war on windows', 1911.

Lady Constance Bulwer-Lytton (1869–1923), having been well treated in prison, exposed the disparity in the treatment of suffragette prisoners when she served a later sentence: this time she assumed the character of Jane Warton, a working-class seamstress, and was force fed.

WSPU volunteers making female prison uniforms for those suffragettes who had been imprisoned to wear on parades, c. 1911.

WSPU Committee Room and Votes for Women newspaper distributors, c. 1911.

Ada Wright, knocked to the ground by the police line in Parliament Square. She was one of many suffragettes who suffered brutality on 'Black Friday', 18 November 1910.

were published in her own book *Prisons and Prisoners* (1914). Suffragettes were left under no illusions with regard to what they would face in prison if they went on hunger strike; some of them endured force feeding ordeals on a number of occasions over several prison sentences. Many of those who had served terms of imprisonment appeared in reconstructed prison uniforms when taking part in suffragette parades.

By 1910 *Votes for Women* was heading towards sales of forty thousand copies a week, with an average weekly readership of 140,000, and its presses and production operations were moved to 156 Charing Cross Road. The WSPU enjoyed a membership of thousands and employed 110 salaried staff; supported by an army of volunteers, they organised large demonstrations, exhibitions and processions and produced campaign and propaganda material. However, the self-proclaimed 'Law-Abiding Suffragists' of the NUWSS retained the majority of the support of the women's movement with some fifty thousand members, and although most suffragist women's groups continued to campaign for votes by legal means, their efforts remain overshadowed as media attention was drawn towards the escalating militant actions of the WSPU suffragettes.

Elizabeth Garrett Anderson and Emmeline Pankhurst shortly after they were allowed to pass through the police line in Parliament Square on 18 November 1910.

With the general election of 1910 looming, Mrs Pankhurst declared a truce because she wanted the government to decide what they would do about the votes for women issue 'in an atmosphere of peace and calm.' The result was the 1910 Conciliation Bill, which would extend the franchise to wealthy, property-owning women in Britain and Ireland. Despite support from the Liberal government, the bill did not get the necessary backing because many Liberal and Conservative MPs feared the negative impact on their parties during general elections. The bill failed and on Friday 18 November the WSPU sent a delegation of about three hundred women to march on Parliament. They were met by a cordon of police; Emmeline Pankhurst and Elizabeth Garrett Anderson were allowed through but the rest of the contingent were forcibly driven back. Journalist and suffragist campaigner Henry Nevinson described the scene:

> At the front the struggle was then both piteous and horrible. Against the gathering lines of police the women charged again and again with reckless indifference to the blows or violent pushes that flung them to the ground. Indeed the whole length of the street from the official residences down to the entrance was now one wild turmoil of struggling men and women.

It was reported that a number of the women suffered punches to their faces, breasts and shoulders but that they 'instinctively tidied themselves' and went back again and again – some women were seen to be thrown down as many as three or four times. After six hours of 'battle', 119 had been arrested; many were released the following day but the newspapers sided with the suffragettes. Photographs of police assaulting and manhandling unarmed

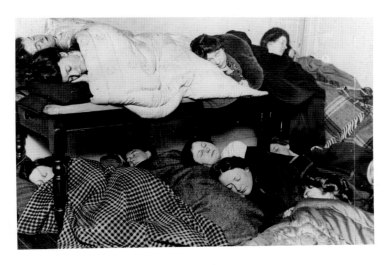

One of many groups of suffragettes subverting the 1911 census statistics by holding a sleep-over.

33

Illustrated London News artist's impression of suffragettes smashing shop windows in the West End on 1 March 1912. About 150 suffragettes, armed with toffee hammers and stones, caused damage to 270 premises. More than 220 suffragettes were arrested.

One of the toffee hammers carried by suffragettes to smash windows.

women protestors spelled a public relations disaster for the government and gained massive sympathy and public concern for the suffragettes. No one was killed outright but many were injured, some seriously, among them Ellen Pitfield, who died of incurable injuries sustained in the mêlée. The day was soon dubbed 'Black Friday' and as far as the WSPU was concerned the truce was over.

The following year, in April 1911, the census was to be taken and the WSPU saw a great opportunity to subvert the value of the survey by either refusing to fill in the census papers, an act that could result in a £5 fine or a month's imprisonment, or evading the enumerators by staying away from home. Many suffragettes chose the latter, safer, option and attended specially staged concerts and entertainments before retiring in groups to sleep-overs. Some suffragettes also got up to mischief, for example Emily Wilding Davison, who hid herself in a cupboard in the Palace of Westminster overnight so that on the census form she could legitimately give her place of residence as the 'House of Commons'. On the whole event, Emmeline Pankhurst recorded: 'Mr John Burns, who as head of the Local Government Board was responsible for the census, decided to treat the affair with magnanimity.'

The second attempt to introduce the Conciliation Bill failed again in 1911, but Prime Minister Asquith changed his position relating to women's suffrage, announcing that the government would introduce a bill in the next session to provide universal male suffrage, which would be capable of amendment by Parliament to give some women the vote, should Parliament support it. Both suffragists and suffragettes felt there were now 'friends in the Cabinet'; a number of ministers were speaking openly in favour of votes for women and real hopes were raised for the success of the bill. The debate was delayed until March and, sensing another let-down, militant suffragettes could contain their frustation no longer and spontaneously began what soon

Below left: Handbill for the Women's Coronation Procession, 1911.

Below right: Pro-suffragette cartoon postcard, c. 1910, part of *The House that Man Built* series, based on the rhyme 'The House that Jack Built'. The 'House' referred to is Parliament.

VOTES FOR WOMEN
Women's Coronation
PROCESSION
(Five miles long).
Saturday, June 17th,
START 5.30 P.M.
Route via:—TRAFALGAR SQUARE,
PALL MALL, PICCADILLY,
KNIGHTSBRIDGE.
70 BANDS!
1,000 BANNERS!

THE PROCESSION will march to Kensington, where great meetings in the ROYAL ALBERT HALL and in the EMPRESS ROOMS will be held by the Women's Social and Political Union, at 8.30 p.m., in support of the Women Suffrage Bill.

Speakers:
Mrs. PANKHURST, Mrs. PETHICK LAWRENCE, Miss VIDA GOLDSTEIN, Miss CHRISTABEL PANKHURST, and others.

Tickets for the Meeting in the EMPRESS ROOMS for Numbered and Reserved Seats, price 2s. 6d. and 1s., can be obtained from The Ticket Secretary, W.S.P.U., 4, Clements Inn, W.C.

For all further plans and particulars read the weekly newspaper VOTES FOR WOMEN. (Price One Penny.) It can be obtained at all newsagents and bookstalls.

Printed by Dr. Clements Press, Limited, Portugal Street, Kingsway, London, W.C.

FROM PRISON
TO CITIZENSHIP

This is "THE HOUSE" that man built;
And this is the Flag of the Woman's Franchise,
Which is making our Ministers open their eyes:
Fighting with grit, to the front bit by bit;
Determined in Parliament one day to sit,
The bold Suffragette who is sure to get yet
Into "THE HOUSE" that man built.

became a 'war on windows', during which shops and department stores across the country suffered a great deal of damage through stone throwing and hammer attack on their windows. In London, indiscriminate damage to windows of businesses occurred along Regent Street, Piccadilly and the Strand in the West End, and, in a daring raid, windows were smashed even on Downing Street.

The third attempt to pass the Conciliation Bill was finally defeated on 28 March 1912 by 208 to 222. The suffragettes felt not only that they had been let down again but a number of ministers had reneged on promises of support when it actually came to the vote. For the suffragettes, it was the final straw and they not only returned to but also escalated their militant action. In the wake of the window attacks Emmeline Pankhurst was given two months' imprisonment for her part in the window-smashing campaign and Christabel Pankhurst, her mother's loyal militant general, already known as 'The Queen of the Mob', became a woman wanted by the Metropolitan Police Criminal Investigation Department 'For conspiracy,

The Women's Coronation Procession, 17 June 1911, a week before the coronation of George V, was organised by the WSPU to enlist the support of the new king for the Conciliation Bill of 1911.

procuring, aiding and abetting persons to commit offences under Section 51 of the Malicious Damage to Property Act'; her image and description were published in *The Police Gazette*. She had already fled the country to a self-imposed exile in Paris. Command of the WSPU was taken by the loyal Annie Kenney, who made weekly trips to see Christabel in France.

Christabel continued to plan new strategies for the WSPU and devised its most dramatic militant action to date while she was in exile – the arson campaign on both public and private property. Frederick and Emmeline Pethick-Lawrence went to France to try to dissuade Christabel from this new escalation, fearing the loss of supporters and public sympathy for the WSPU. Emmeline had been released from prison and was with Christabel; both mother and daughter made it clear they resented any questioning of their new plans. Christabel had been uncomfortable about the involvement of any men in the WSPU for some time and, despite all they had done for the cause, both Pethick-

Excerpt from *The Police Gazette* showing the CID 'wanted' notice for Christabel Pankhurst, 22 March 1912.

Cover of *The Police Gazette* for 22 March 1912.

The acid attacks on golf courses were satirised in the *Punch* cartoon 'Acidulated Golf', published on 23 February 1913.

ACIDULATED GOLF.

"DON'T KNOW HOW TO PLAY THIS, CADDIE?"

"WHY, YOU'VE GOT A GRAND LINE, SIR. FOLLOW THE S. THE OTHER GENTLEMAN'S BUNKERED IN THE E."

Part of the destruction caused by the suffragette arson attack on Kew Gardens in 1913.

Lawrences were expelled from the Union; Christabel organised a replacement newspaper entitled *The Suffragette* and the WSPU proceeded with the arson campaign.

Sporadic instances of fire-starting by suffragettes occurred from the summer of 1912 and by 1913 the arson campaign had gathered momentum. It took a number of forms: suffragettes armed with bottles of acid would watch General Post Office pillar boxes and when these became full of mail the suffragette would tip the contents of her bottle through the slot or set it on fire. Acid was also used to scorch 'Votes for Women' slogans upon the greens of golf courses, while many more serious arson attacks were staged, damaging or completely destroying a number of railway stations, cricket pavilions, racecourse stands, pleasure piers, hotels, golf clubhouses, country houses and even churches in incidents all over the country. Incendiary devices were also intercepted in the post addressed to Lloyd George and the Prime Minister.

With so many instances of criminal damage committed by suffragettes, unprecedented numbers of them were ending up in prison, including Emmeline and Sylvia Pankhurst. A number of suffragettes went on hunger strike and were force fed – but the protests the 'torture' procedure caused in the media were counterproductive: as a consequence the Home Office rushed through a raft of special measures that soon became the Prisoner's (Temporary Discharge of Ill Health) Act (1913), commonly known to the suffragettes as the 'Cat and Mouse Act'. It permitted the release of prisoners on hunger strike until they had recovered sufficiently – then enforced their readmission to complete their sentence.

The WSPU capitalised on the public outrage at the force feeding of suffragette prisoners with this dramatic 'Torturing Women in Prison' poster, c. 1913.

For many, the most memorable and poignant moment of the entire women's suffrage campaign occurred on Derby Day, 4 June 1913. Emily Wilding Davison did not intend to become a martyr. She had purchased a return rail ticket and a ticket to a suffragette dance later that day but had gone to the Derby and had intended simply to fasten WSPU colours to the King's horse, Anmer, so it would finish the race flying them. Film footage of the incident shows Emily bob under the rail at Tattenham Corner carrying the banner of the WSPU and walk calmly up the course towards the

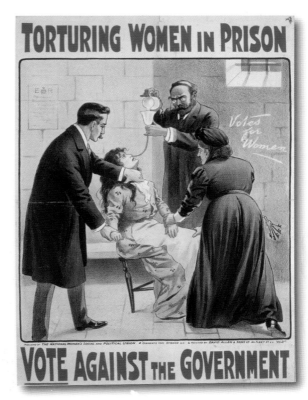

Right: This incisive *Punch* cartoon captures the mood at the height of militant suffragette activity. 'The Majesty of the Law' was published on 5 March 1913.

Below: Emily Wilding Davison (1872–1913), the suffragette 'martyr'.

Bottom: The tragic aftermath on Tattenham Corner, Derby Day, 4 June 1913.

thundering hooves of the horses; she reaches up to grab the bridle of Anmer as it draws up to her, the horse strikes her with its chest and then turns a somersault. The horse fell, knocking Davison to the ground, unconscious; the King's jockey, Herbert Jones, suffered mild concussion. Removed to Epsom Cottage Hospital, Emily died four days later from a fractured skull and internal injuries caused by the incident. She was buried with full suffragette honours, her funeral procession passing through the streets of London on 14 June 1913. Emily's coffin was then sent by train and she was laid to rest in her family plot in the churchyard of St Mary the Virgin, Morpeth, on 15 June. Her gravestone bears the WSPU slogan 'Deeds not words'.

Arrest of suffragette Ethel Cox at a protest in London, October 1913.

The funeral procession of Emily Davison with full suffragette honours, 14 June 1913.
(IWM Q 81834)

THE GREAT WAR

A S THE YEAR 1914 APPROACHED, the world stage was a turbulent one and it appeared a matter of when rather than if there was going to be a war. The militant WSPU campaigns carried on but all was not well in the leadership of the organisation and the Pankhursts began drawing in their horns. Sylvia had worked tirelessly to represent and lead the working-class women in the WSPU and maintained strong socialist links and personal beliefs; Christabel, however, did not like the way she concentrated her efforts on the East End of London and conducted the campaign for votes for women along class lines, believing this discredited the WSPU. Sylvia would not compromise and her East London Federation of Suffragettes was terminated as a branch of the WSPU and became a separate organisation. Although this never blossomed into a significant suffrage organisation, Sylvia continued her work for working-class suffrage and founded her own paper, the *Women's Dreadnought*.

Opposite: Mrs Pankhurst was carried from Buckingham Palace by a policeman while trying to present a petition to King George V on 21 May 1914.

Left: Sylvia Pankhurst addressing a crowd outside the headquarters of the East London Federation of Suffragettes, Old Ford Road, Bow, November 1912.

Fire started by
suffragettes at
Britannia Pier,
Great Yarmouth,
Norfolk on
17 April 1914.

BRITANNIA PIER FIRE (17ᵗʰ APRIL 1914) GT YARMOUTH.

The militant campaign of the suffragettes intensified yet again in 1914. Over the seven months up to and including July there were no fewer than 107 recorded suffragette acts of arson, including the firing of Britannia Pier at Great Yarmouth and the destruction of the Bath House Hotel at Felixstowe. The event that drew the national headlines, however, was a new strand of destruction – the mutilation of works of art, most infamously the attack carried out by Mary Richardson (alias Polly Dick) with an axe upon the Rokeby *Venus* in the National Gallery in March, followed by another attack upon Clausen's *Primavera* at the Royal Academy in May. In total, some eleven acts of mutilation of works of art, combined with fourteen other incidents of suffragette militant destruction, had caused damage in excess of £250,000 in 1914 alone.

It was also in May 1914 that the WSPU made a final resolution to present a direct petition to the King. The petition argued the following:

1. To demand votes for women
2. To protest against torture (force feeding of hunger strikers in prison)
3. To claim equal treatment for the militant Ulster men and militant suffragists.

Leaflets promoting the event urged people to remember Black Friday and come to see that the women's deputation was 'not assaulted by the police on approaching Buckingham Palace'. The deputation, led by Mrs Pankhurst and marching towards Buckingham Palace, numbered hundreds of women on the afternoon of 21 May 1914 and drew a massive crowd which lined the route.

Suffragette fire at Breadsall church, near Derby, 5 June 1914.

At the gates of the palace some women threw eggs filled with coloured powder while others tried to climb the railings. Police on foot and on horseback engaged the women, and a violent struggle ensued in which over sixty women were arrested. Emmeline, having almost reached the front of the palace, was grabbed from behind by a burly police officer and carried off as she called out: 'Arrested at the gates of the palace – tell the King.' The photograph of this incident was widely published and has become one of the most iconic images of the women's suffrage movement. The march on Buckingham Palace proved to be the last mass demonstration of the Women's Suffrage Movement, for, a

The aftermath of the suffragette arson attack on the Bath Hotel, Felixstowe, on 28 April 1914, which caused £23,000 of damage.

Vesta matches, the favoured fire starter of suffragettes.

few days after war was declared on 4 August 1914, the WSPU announced the suspension of its militant action to give their support to the war effort.

Emmeline Pankhurst spoke in favour of Lord Kitchener's appeal for recruits, calling men to join up and fight 'on behalf of women'. Many of the activists in the suffrage movement immediately set about establishing units to support British troops but were treated with disdain by the War Office, irrespective of their associations with the suffrage cause – simply because they were women.

The first in the field were prominent suffragettes Decima Moore and the Hon Evelina Haverfield, who raised the Women's Emergency Corps to provide feeding centres for soldiers and refugees. Then came the Women's Volunteer Reserve, sponsored by the Marchioness of Londonderry, the Marchioness of Titchfield and the Countess of Pembroke and Montgomery; there was even Mrs Dawson Scott's Women's Defence Relief Corps. Some units were already long-established: the First Aid Nursing Yeomanry (FANY), raised in 1907, included a number of suffragettes and suffragists; and the Women's Sick and Wounded Convoy Corps, raised by the redoubtable suffragist Mrs Mabel St Clair Stobart, which had done good service during the Balkan War in 1912. The Women's Hospital Corps, raised by Dr Flora Murray and Louisa Garrett Anderson, was raised in September 1914. All of these units offered their services, voluntarily and freely, to the War Office,

A British Red Cross Society and Order of St John of Jerusalem Voluntary Aid Detachment driver and her ambulance, 1917.

but the reaction they all received is typified by that expressed directly to Edinburgh surgeon Elsie Inglis, founder of another early all-female unit, the Scottish Women's Hospitals, when she was granted a meeting at Whitehall in August 1914. After explaining her proposal, she was told by the official: 'My good lady, go home and sit still – no petticoats here.' Undaunted, these well-connected women used their contacts to persuade diplomats and the military of Britain's foreign allies they were welcome to support troops in Belgium, France and Serbia.

It was to prove to be a struggle for women to 'do their bit' during the First World War. Although seventy thousand women registered themselves for work at the request of the Board of Trade, only two thousand had been called for national service. Both suffrage societies and suffragettes were frustrated by a failure to utilise their full potential as a willing and able workforce. There was no doubting their resolve and patriotism: in 1915 Christabel changed her newspaper's name from *The Suffragette* to *Britannia* and campaigned ardently to do more for the war effort. However, it was a combination of events that fully mobilised women into munitions work.

A group of munitions workers – proud to be known as 'Munitionettes', 1916.

As women became more liberated through their war work, women's sports teams (notably, as seen here, football teams) flourished and even played their matches in public – unthinkable before the war!

Right: A member of the Women's Land Army during the First World War. Between her coat and her boots and buskins may be seen her breeches – another wartime first for women.

Far right: Violet Jackson, a village postwoman, employed by the General Post Office 'for the duration'.

First and foremost came the 'Shells Scandal' of 1915, which was exposed after the startling revelation that in the opinion of Sir John French, the British Commander-in-Chief, a shortage of munitions had led directly to the failure of the British offensive at Neuve Chapelle in March 1915. The Liberal Chancellor, David Lloyd George, fervently believed radical improvements were required in the munitions industry if Britain was to carry on a prolonged war against Germany. The 'Shells Scandal' became a key factor in the fall of the Liberal Government in May 1915 and the establishment of a new coalition in which the new Ministry of Munitions was created under Lloyd George.

The second factor was a renewed appeal to women to serve. Lloyd George met with Emmeline Pankhurst and brokered a deal in which over £4,000 of funds was provided by the Treasury towards the cost of WSPU staff organising the 'Call to Women' march through London on 17 July 1915. thirty thousand women marched, bands played, and banners were carried emblazoned with the slogan 'We Demand the Right to Serve' – it looked very much like a suffrage march from pre-war years but instead of purple, white and green the colours were red, white and blue; the crowds cheered and there was no fracas with the police.

With the Board of Trade now actively seeking placements, thousands of women went to work in factories and businesses; many local firms also recruited women under their own initiatives. The WSPU, NUWSS and other pre-war women's suffrage groups kept active through the war, carrying on the patriotic ethos and fighting for better working conditions and equal pay for women, and continued to press for the enfranchisement of wom

During 1917, as the First World War rolled on through bloody campaigns on the Western Front, the enfranchisement of all male householders, all servicemen, and women aged thirty and above with property was brought to parliament. Lloyd George was now Prime Minister and summed up the situation by stating: 'the heroic patriotism of the women workers during the war had now made their claim irresistible.' The Qualification of Women clause in the Representation of the People Act was passed by the House of Commons in December (by a massive 364 votes to 23), and by the House of Lords in January 1918, and became law on 6 February 1918. By this time women had taken the place of men in many jobs that would have been seen as totally unacceptable employment for women in the years before the First World War. Many had filled the massive requirement for munitions workers and many others were serving in uniform on farms in the Women's Land Army and in non-combatant roles, 'freeing a man for the front' in uniformed units in all three military services.

And above all, when the general election was called on 14 December 1918, for the first time in legal and political history, a significant number of women had the right to vote.

Doing 'their bit' at the front, First Aid Nursing Yeomanry drivers attached to the Belgian Army at Calais on 8 May 1918.

AT LAST!

AFTERMATH AND LEGACY

THE 1918 ELECTION SAW WOMEN'S SUFFRAGE ORGANISATIONS delighted to have obtained their first tranche of women voters; seventeen women stood for election and Nancy Astor was elected, thus becoming the first woman to sit in the House of Commons as a Member of Parliament.

Times were changing: the men who returned from the First World War returned to the jobs that had been done by women in wartime. More women were fulfilling jobs and roles in public life than before the war; however, most married women went back to their homes, happy to look to the future, settle down and start families – but they also looked to enjoy more structured and valuable activities outside the home. Some continued to serve or became new members of organisations such as the British Red Cross Society and St John Ambulance, which provided voluntary nursing services to the general public. Above all, the greatest expansion of membership was enjoyed by the Women's Institute. The WI had been established in Britain during the First World War but in peace time presented a useful, entertaining and well-structured organisation for women. It was a most remarkable organisation, for its membership was inclusive and broke down many social barriers: from the lady of the manor to domestic servants, housewives to shop workers, all could join and were urged to work together to become active members of society.

The ethos among women's groups in the 1920s emphasised welfare feminism, and the WSPU faded away while groups such as the NUWSS reacted to changing times and embraced the new challenges. It changed its name to the National Union of Societies for Equal Citizenship (NUSEC) and campaigned for social reforms, notably a family allowance for married women who cared for their children at home. There was still dissent and many feminists viewed the new emphasis on welfare as coming at the expense of sexual equality. A number of pressure groups, such as the Equal Pay Campaign Committee and the Association for Moral and Social Hygiene, emerged to fight single-issue campaigns; umbrella organisations, such as the National Council for Women and the National Union

Opposite: The first step on the road to equal franchise heralded by the *Punch* cartoon 'At Last!', published on 23 January 1918.

PUNCH, OR THE LONDON CHARIVARI—MAY 23, 1928.

THE DIE-HARD
(FEATURING LORD BANBURY).
AN ITEM OMITTED FROM THE ROYAL TOURNAMENT (BY REQUEST).

The surge of support for the Equal Franchise Bill could not be held back any longer, even by the entrenched 'die-hards' in the House of Lords, as illustrated in this *Punch* cartoon from 23 May 1928.

of Societies for Equal Citizenship (NUSEC), soon sprang up to combine efforts in shared and allied goals.

The women's qualification clause in the Representation of the People Act (1918) granted the right to vote to women who fulfilled age and property qualifications. The next challenge was to extend the vote to include all women. The first moves towards this were instigated by the NUSEC; an Equal Franchise Special Committee was instigated in 1920 including co-opted members of the Federation of Women Civil Servants, Association of Women Clerks and Secretaries, Catholic Women's Suffrage Society and Women's Freedom League (WFL), who would apply pressure for the extension through peaceful means.

By contrast, the Six Point Group (SPG), founded by Lady Rhondda in 1921, had six specific aims:

1. Satisfactory legislation on child assault
2. Satisfactory legislation for the widowed mother
3. Satisfactory legislation for the unmarried mother and her child
4. Equal rights of guardianship for married parents
5. Equal pay for teachers
6. Equal opportunities for men and women in the civil service

Many of the members of the SPG were ex-WSPU members and demanded rapid change by 'making themselves apparent, and if need be so unpleasant, to the powers that be that they decide to give them what they ask'.

Despite a number of calls from the SPG for a return to militant action, the peaceful yet persistent pressure applied predominantly by NUSEC and WFL (bolstered by many other groups that gave their names in support of them and joined their rallies) won through and at long last the Representation of the People (Equal Franchise) Bill was introduced in March 1928. The Bill was passed at its second reading by a majority of 377 and received Royal Assent on 2 July 1928. Finally, women had achieved equal voting rights to men.

Many of the senior women of the suffrage and suffragette movements continued their active participation in politics and went on to champion numerous social and women's causes for many years afterwards. We should never forget the debt of gratitude society owes to them; despite being supremely strong of will, many of their bodies were prematurely weakened and their lives cut short through their fight for votes for women.

The health of Emmeline Pankhurst, the woman who came to symbolise the votes for women cause, was severely affected by her hunger strikes. She retired from public life after the war and went to France to run a tea shop, but unfortunately the bitter winters there were not good for her health and she returned home. Her old gastric complaint returned and, unable to retain food, Emmeline faded fast – she died aged sixty-nine on 14 June 1928. In 1999 *Time Magazine* named Emmeline Pankhurst as one of the hundred most important people of the twentieth century and went on to state: '... she shaped an idea of women for our time; she shook society into a new pattern from which there could be no going back.'

Nancy Astor (1879–1964), the first woman to sit in Parliament.

Suffragettes gather together to mark the tenth anniversary of the first franchise for women. Front row, left to right: Mrs Edith Mansell Moullin, Mrs Emmeline Pethick-Lawrence, Miss Sylvia Pankhurst, Mrs How-Martin, Mrs Anna Munro, Mrs Bull, Mrs Nina Boyle, Miss Daisy Solomon, Miss Elsa Gye.

FURTHER READING

Abrams, Fran. *Freedom's Cause: The Lives of the Suffragettes*. Profile Books, 2003.

Adams, Jad. *Pankhurst*. Haus Publishing, 2003.

Atkinson, Diane. *Suffragettes in the Purple, White & Green: London 1906–14*. Museum of London, 1992.

Atkinson, Diane. *The Suffragettes in Pictures*. History Press, 2010.

Bartley, Paula. *Votes for Women 1860–1928*. Hodder Murray, 2003.

Crawford, Elizabeth. *The Women's Suffrage Movement*. Routledge, 1999.

Fulford, Roger. *Votes for Women: The Story of a Struggle*. Faber, 1957.

Harrison, Shirley. *Sylvia Pankhurst: A Maverick Life, 1882–1960*. Aurum, 2004.

Law, Cheryl. *Suffrage and Power: The Women's Movement, 1918–1928*. Tauris, 1997.

Lewis, Jane (editor). *Before the Vote was Won: Arguments For and Against Women's Suffrage, 1864–1896*. Routledge & Kegan Paul, 1987.

Liddington, Jill, and Norris, Jill. *One Hand Tied Behind Us*. Virago, 1978.

Lytton, Constance, and Warton, Jane. *Prisons and Prisoners: Some Personal Experiences*. Heinemann, 1914.

'Unity is strength!' – a postcard from the height of the suffragette campaign showing all classes of women united in the cause of Votes for Women, c. 1912.

Unity is strength!

Votes for Women.

Mackenzie, Midge. *Shoulder to Shoulder*. Knopf, 1975.

Marcus, Jane (editor). *Suffrage and the Pankhursts*. Routledge and Kegan Paul, 1987.

Marlow, Joyce (editor). *Votes for Women: The Virago Book of Suffragettes*. Virago, 2001.

Mayer, Annette. *Women in Britain 1900–2000*. Hodder & Stoughton, 2002.

Pankhurst, Christabel. *Unshackled*. Hutchinson, 1959.

Pankhurst, Emmeline. *My Own Story*. Eveleigh Nash, 1914; Virago, 1979.

Pankhurst, Sylvia. *The Suffragette Movement*. Longman, 1931.

Phillips, Melanie. *The Ascent of Woman: A History of the Suffragette Movement*. Abacus, 2004.

Pugh, Martin. *Women and the Women's Suffrage Movement in Britain 1914–1959*. Macmillan, 1992.

Pugh, Martin. *The March of Women*. Oxford University Press, 2000.

Raeburn, Antonia. *The Militant Suffragettes*. Michael Joseph, 1973.

Rendall, Jane (editor). *Equal or Different: Women's Politics, 1800–1914*. Blackwell, 1987.

Rosen, Andrew. *Rise Up, Women!* Routledge & Kegan Paul, 1974.

Rover, Constance. *Women's Suffrage and Party Politics in Britain, 1866–1914*. Routledge & Kegan Paul, 1967.

Storey, Neil R., and Housego, Molly. *Women in the First World War*. Shire, 2010.

Alice Stewart Kerr's WSPU prisoner's certificate, c. 1913.

INDEX